SAM THE LANDSCAPE ARCHITECT

An Environmental Design Story

by Shannon Gapp

Illustrated by Lime Valley Advertising, Inc.

BOLTON & MENK
Real People. Real Solutions.

Esri Press
REDLANDS | CALIFORNIA

This is Samantha.
She goes by Sam.

Sam knows she can **design** parks with a **plan**.

Sam likes to color and
Sam likes to draw.

Sam likes to plant
trees that are big and
trees that are small.

Sam loves to play and Sam loves to run.
That is why Sam creates parks that are just so much fun.

Sam likes to walk
and Sam likes to talk.

So Sam creates paths she can draw on with chalk.

Sam loves the city
and Sam loves her trike.

So Sam designs roads
with a lane just for bikes.

Sam plays with dogs
and Sam likes to
look at art.

So Sam designed her very own dog play park.

Sam designs splash pads and playgrounds galore.

Sam even restores prairies and wetlands
and forests to explore.

Sam knows she wants
to create even more.
She wants to design
street corners and benches
and all things outdoors.

Sam creates **pollinator** gardens for butterflies and bees. She even creates sensory gardens you can smell, touch, hear, and see.

Sam designs gardens for hospitals that help heal. She also creates **community gardens** that give neighbors a meal.

Sam loves the water and thinks pollution is mean.

So Sam designs **rain gardens** that help keep our rivers and lakes clean.

Sam loves
climbing trees
and playing
in leaves.

There's nothing she would love more
than a world full of trees.

When Sam grows up she wants her ideas to be seen.
She plans to be a **Landscape Architect**—
to make the world green.

Glossary

Community Gardens – Plots of land gardened collectively by residents with the aim of growing locally sourced fruits and vegetables.

Design – The act of drawing or sketching how a place or object could look.

Landscape Architect — A person who creates places for enjoyment through design and plantings.

Landscape Architecture — The practice of improving an outdoor space through planning, planting, and construction.

Plan -- A drawing that shows how something should be built.

Pollinator — An insect or animal that carries pollen from one plant to another to create more flowers, fruit, and food.

Pollution — Environmental contamination by waste, chemicals, and other harmful substances.

Rain Garden — A garden that collects rainwater from sidewalks, roads, and other surfaces to improve nearby streams and lakes.

Splash Pad — A play area with water and sprinklers.

Also available from STEAM at Work!

Learn more at go.esri.com/samlovesdesigning.